Schoolboy to Soldier

Schoolboy to Soldier

by

Dennis Hamilton

Basiljet Books

Hampshire, UK

First published in the UK by Basiljet Books

This edition © Dennis Hamilton, 2013

The moral rights of the author have been asserted.

This book is sold subject to the condition that it shall not, by way of trade or otherwise, be lent, re-sold, hired out, or otherwise circulated without the publisher's prior consent in any form of binding or cover than that which it is published and without a similar condition including this condition being imposed on the subsequent purchaser.

ISBN 978-0-955847813

Jam and Bridges

BORN A WAR BABY (just!) in January 1945, I spent my first five years in a mining village called North Seaton Colliery on the north bank of the river Wansbeck. Son of a miner, John (known as "Jackie" to his mining colleagues), and a hard working mother, Jane ("Ginny"), I had four siblings: one sister, Joyce, and three brothers, Raymond, Julian, and Barry (in age order). Another sister, Jane, was to follow four years later. The greater family lived in what has now become known as "The Borders," some in Scotland, the others - mine included - in Northumberland. We lived in what were called the Middle Doubles, rows of terraced mining houses which, although basic, were warm, dry and fairly comfortable. The rows were separated by unsurfaced lanes which became a mud bath at any sign of inclement weather. Each house consisted of three upstairs bedrooms, a dining/sitting room, parlour and kitchen. The toilet was next to the coal house outside in the back yard and had no light or heat of any description. I now know why this was often called the throne room as my father had erected a small shelf just high enough to reach whilst sitting on "the throne." This was to hold his pint mug of tea whilst he contemplated world issues. Toilet paper was very rare indeed and usually supplemented by carefully cut up pages of the *Daily Mirror* threaded with string and hung on a nail. Trips to and from the toilet could be a bit of an expedition (especially in the winter months).

The only heating in the house came from the big coal fire in the dining/sitting room, so bedtimes were rather nippy and hot water bottles were a godsend. Father used to shower daily at the mine after his shift whilst the rest of us had to make do with the tin bath (which used to hang on a nail outside in the back yard) in front of the fire, filled with kettles full of hot water from the kitchen. This was usually followed by sitting at mother's knee while she checked our hair with a comb and brown paper to catch any signs of anything untoward. Life was hard but as kids everything from the raggy short trousers to the boots on our feet was taken with a pinch of salt because only a few in the village were any better off.

Food, although not plentiful, was always good, and fights over who was having the crust of the bread were a common practice. I, being the youngest, only won when Mum or Dad intervened. One way to subsidise our food was of course by fishing, not in the conventional manner with rod and line but with a garden cane with a six inch nail attached to one end. Walking along the sandbanks on the river as the tide was either ebbing or flowing and feeling the *dabs* (flatfish) under bare feet, you then placed the six inch nail between the big and second toe, pushed down piercing the fish. Once a few were caught they were then taken home to be fried and eaten with bread and margarine.

Down a small lane, hidden from view of the rest of the village by an embankment, were three or four beautiful cottages – privately owned I think, perhaps by mine officials and their families. Opposite these was the North Seaton Rowing club house. This contained a number of what we termed *skiffs*, which were two, four or eight-manned racing rowing boats similar to the ones used in the Olympics today. These provided some entertainment usually at weekends, although I doubt many of the miners actually took part in the rowing itself. Further along the riverbank, many of the miners and others from the near vicinity had moorings for their small fishing boats. Moorings were usually homemade with small wooden sheds, and as a whole always looked in some need of refurbishment as did a lot of the small sailing craft. Prized possessions they were, however, as it gave people a means of escape from living and breathing the coal dust inherent in their jobs. Thinking back, weekends must have been a godsend to the miners, although even these could be marred with having to attend for shift work on a Sunday evening. I asked my dad one day why he and other miners always seemed to take jam sandwiches in their bait boxes (lunch boxes) when they went to work. The short answer was that it was the only thing they could taste when down on the coal face. Jam sandwiches for all those years – no wonder the coal dust used to stick to their lungs.

∞ ∞ ∞ ∞ ∞

The Black Bridge

THE RIVER WANSBECK WAS a real source of enjoyment and adventure for us young children – not just for the fishing, but also because of the sand dunes that allowed us to play what were then normal war games or Cowboys and Indians. Not far from the river estuary, behind the sand dunes, was the council tip. It was hidden away, but easily accessible to those with an enquiring mind in search of old broken toys or useful objects that had been thrown away because they were considered to be no longer of any value.

Ever the hunter-gatherer, it was soon found, at low tide, that the holes in the river banks contained eating crabs. I harvested these with the aid of a hook on the end of a wooden pole.

Two bridges crossed the river within easy reach of North Seaton: the Trot (this was where the tubs full of coal crossed the river en route to the nearby Cambois Power Station), and The Black Railway Bridge. Fortunately, my parents never found out that one of the silly things we used to do as kids was to cross the river underneath The Black Bridge, climbing over the metal stays and girders as we went. A fall of sixty or so feet into the river would have had some serious consequences. The Trot, on the other hand, was a piece of cake! Using the tubs themselves as a means of transport, only the occasional mine worker had to be avoided. The mere fact that the steel hawsers to which the tubs were attached were dangerous was not even taken into consideration. What was it all about? Well, why did the chicken cross the road?

The Black Bridge (with some renovation)

On Water

SUNDAYS SOON BECAME a family favourite (although the workload on my mother was tremendous) – early fried breakfast, out to play, and then back in for Sunday Dinner (the joint of meat had been slow roasting over the previous night). Meat, vegetables, Yorkshire pudding and gravy followed, normally, by rice pudding (with jam). For some reason, only my father had half a Yorkshire pudding with his rice, a habit that none of my siblings ever seemed to follow. Now I know through similar experiences with my own children how difficult it must have been for my mother to get me to eat vegetables, even to the point of mixing things like swede in with the mashed potatoes. During all this, my poor mother would be baking pies and pastries in preparation for the Sunday tea. This was attended by Grandma Bell and my favourite relative, Uncle Jim (who was, not wholly, but severely handicapped with his sight). Arriving well before tea was due, a game of cards would commence (only for adults) with gambling for stakes of a penny or halfpenny. Tea would then commence with the table laid with all sorts of home-baked goodies, and the children would sit and watch the adults (who appeared to be scoffing the lot) enjoying their food. (Of course, mum used to keep some back in the kitchen but it was all part of the Sunday ritual). It was not unusual for the odd couple of pence or so to fall into my hands from someone (usually Uncle Jim) especially if he was on a winning streak.

The village amenities (as I remember them) were somewhat scarce and consisted of the following: one co-op (which was a furniture and general provisions store); a fish and chip shop; two schools (infants/juniors and senior); and, the institute which in itself comprised of a dance hall, bar room, snooker rooms (and other places kids weren't allowed to trespass). Outside, it had tennis courts and a bowling green. (I suppose someone must have used them although I never actually remember seeing anyone). I also have vague recollections of a back street house where sweets could be purchased for the odd penny or so. One unusual thing that the village mine possessed, fortunately for me, was its own ambulance. Coloured green, it was kept in a wooden type garage on the outskirts. I say fortunately for me because around my fourth birthday I suffered from a burst appendix which was caused by me scraping out Fussels condensed milk tins after my mother had finished with them. I don't believe it was the milk that caused the problem but rather the inner lining of the can. A rather lengthy stay and operation in Newcastle's Royal Victoria Hospital followed, of which my abiding memory was of a large green wooden aeroplane that I really fell in love with and wanted to take home with me. Belonging to the hospital, of course the aeroplane had to be left behind much to my chagrin but my father being a jack of all trades actually melted some lead and cast me a metal one in its place.

∞ ∞ ∞ ∞ ∞

At the Mine

ON A FRIDAY, DEPENDING ON WHICH SHIFT my Dad was on, he would take me along to wait in the queue at the mining office for that week's pay. Here I would stand with the other miners, who looked hard and tired. The muck seemed ingrained as did the Wills Woodbine cigarette that was always hanging from their bottom lips. Wives (with their hair covered in a scarf and pinned so that it looked like a turban) took their place in the line if husbands were down the pit. Miner's wives are as hardworking as their menfolk – busy at home cleaning, cooking, washing, and generally trying to make ends meet, but seemingly always with a smile on their faces regardless of living in the constant fear of hearing the mine's alarm system and the bad news that may follow. The mine: life saver and life taker. Sometimes on rare occasions children were allowed (probably not officially) the rare privilege of eating in the mine canteen. A minimal charge was made, and I think this was probably the precursor to me enjoying my military meals. The mine also had a large stock of carbide, which was used in the miner's headlamps. Dampening the carbide with water produced acetylene gas which could be ignited to produce a dull yellow flame. Boys will be boys, and through experiment it was soon found that bottles stuffed with carbide and thrown into the river produced a mild explosion. Raiding expeditions on the carbide store were exciting and of course being caught usually brought tears to our eyes and a general rubbing with both hands on the affected parts!

A lot of my father's relatives lived in the colliery and visiting my Granny and Grandad Hamilton was an education in itself. Granny in her black dresses with a brightly coloured flowered pinafore always seemed to be either black leading the grate and fireplace or scrubbing the front doorstep. Grandad on the other hand, in his flat cap, blue pin striped suit, and the ever present fob watch and chain, always seemed to be drinking tea out of a saucer. "If it's good enough for Queen Vic hinney, it's good enough for me." One Sunday afternoon, Grandad decided to introduce me to his gambling club. This was held in the Dean – a secluded little valley running down to the river about a mile outside the colliery towards a place called Stakeford. Gambling, what a laugh, two fellows each with a penny balanced on their thumbs would flick them spinning into the air and bets would be placed on which way they landed: heads, tails, or opposites. I can only say no great fortunes were ever made or lost. My abiding memory of that day was that I needed the lavatory urgently and finding a suitable tree settled down only to get my bum stung by a rather large bee. You've got it, watery eyes again.

∞ ∞ ∞ ∞ ∞

New Beginnings

ONE AFTERNOON IN THE AUTUMN OF 1950 I arrived home from school to find my mother in a blaze of excitement. Apparently we had been allocated a brand new semi-detached council house in a place called Spital Crescent, Newbiggin-by-the-Sea. This small fishing and mining town was only four or five miles away, but to a five and half year old boy it seemed like the beginning of a new adventure. Culture shock after culture shock was to rain upon my head in the coming weeks. The house itself comprised of a dining/kitchen, hallway and large sitting room/parlour on the ground floor. Upstairs there were three bedrooms and, wonder upon wonder, an inside bathroom and separate toilet! Further investigation revealed another cupboard, which contained some shelves and a big brass container. This of course was an electric immersion water heater (commonly called the boiler) that supplied hot water throughout the house (kettles were only used for brewing tea from now on). Outside the back door we had an attached brick built shed (quickly commandeered by dad to house his tools), and next to it the coal storage shed. Separate front and rear garden areas with concrete paths completed the wonderment.

Rear garden: what a misnomer that was. It was actually the remains of an overgrown field of heavy clay that the residents cut and tilled to suit their preferences and had little, if any, sign of demarcation between the houses. These gardens still left a great deal of the field untamed, which in turn became a novel playground for us kids. Separating the new council house rear gardens from the older Newbiggin streets was a burn or small stream complete with bushes and a wooden fence on the far bank. Many happy hours were spent tiddler fishing for sticklebacks with garden worms for bait and lines of black cotton and a bent pin. The cut or path at the side of our house led to a small footbridge which again provided a source of entertainment – enabling kids to swing from hand to hand over the burn using the strengthening struts underneath the bridge for support.

Over the burn, almost directly opposite our house, was a small general provisions shop. Again, boys being boys, I found a shortcut to the shop. Rather than taking the path over the bridge, I would jump over the burn through the bushes and over the fence and road into the shop. Accidents will happen, and one misplaced foot usually entailed me arriving at the back door covered in mud and soaking wet. Needless to say, tears, pain, and promises of never doing it again used to follow.

One bright summer's day returning from the little shop via my shortcut, I heard the squawk of a bird in the bushes and looking up found, much to my surprise, a blue budgerigar. I grabbed it and took it home. No claims of ownership seemed forthcoming for the bird, so my Dad at my pleading decided to keep it. No wonder it wasn't claimed, they probably let it go on purpose - what a racket that bird made! I'm almost positive my Dad liberated the bird as its previous owners must have done since it mysteriously disappeared one day when I was at school.

One thing about the move to Newbiggin-by-the-Sea that hadn't occurred to me was the fact that I would have to change schools. And so, it was with some trepidation that I arrived at a larger, more impressive infants' school as the new boy. Shocked to find that pupils didn't use slates and chalk (which had been the norm at my other school) but rather paper and pencils, I had to quickly adapt to this new art. My two abiding remembrances of the infants' school were of Mrs Jobson (the headmistress), a lovely lady; and, one day sitting in class when, outside the window, a large glowing orb of light was seen. Our teacher immediately ordered us to get under our desks.

It was of course ball lightning which exploded with a fearful bang shortly afterwards - but apparently causing little or no damage (apart from a few frayed nerves). I think the most serious problem I had at the junior school was how to become a milk monitor for the class. This was because the milkman in his wisdom always managed to incorporate a bottle or two of orange juice in each crate, which the monitors claimed as their work prizes.

What a difference the move had made to our lives, money was still short (as it was for all miners at that time) and rationing was still in effect for some things. (Sweets were hard to come by). Meat, of course, although more plentiful, was still quite expensive and the cheaper cuts were bought as the norm. One particular dish my mother served up on occasion was a mixture of these cuts: one small lamb chop (for mum), one small piece of liver (for dad), streaky bacon (for the older children) and mince for myself and my younger sister. All this was cooked together with onions and gravy and served up with mashed potatoes and some vegetables. Of course, the smaller cuts of meat and bacon were supplemented with the mince. As I remarked earlier, Sunday's beef roast was always cooked overnight, and I remember on one Sunday we all sat down for lunch only for my mum to find the meat really underdone. It transpired that one of my elder brothers

(Julian), having been out rather late on Saturday night with some of his pals, had invited them back to enjoy some roast beef sandwiches. Later realising the error of his ways he had risen early and replaced the joint with another from the butchers shop, where he worked, hoping no-one would spot the difference. Needless to say Mum, and especially Dad, were not impressed (to say the least).

Newbiggin itself seemed to be a town of three major parts: the posh end (where some people actually owned their own houses); the fisher end (beautiful cottages, where what seemed to be old ladies with clay pipes were always mending fishing nets); and, of course, the colliery end (situated around the mine). The town itself was located around a beautiful sandy bay between two headlands, Church point and the Needles Eye (so called because it had a bridge running over a dip in the land, which made it quite distinct). The town had a thriving coble fishing fleet which like many things gradually disappeared over the years. Fresh fish was never a problem because a large cod could be bought directly from the fishermen for the princely sum of sixpence (around two and a half pence in today's money).

Centrally situated was the town railway station. This was the terminus for trains from Newcastle upon Tyne and was used not only by holiday makers but local people for shopping in other towns along the line. It was also very handy when people wanted to visit the Town Moor (a large entertainment and amusement fair on the outskirts of Newcastle) and of course the Durham Miner's Gala. Fares were relatively cheap but families used to save quite hard to enjoy these once a year trips. Could a boy have had a better place to grow up in? Personally I don't think so.

Although from Cullercoats, this was the type of coble used from Newbiggin-by-the-Sea

Summer and Winter

NO MATTER WHETHER SUMMER OR WINTER, the local area provided the ideal playground for a young boy. The summer brought people crowding onto the beach, and there was some fun in watching them slowly pushed back towards the promenade by the incoming sea. Another of the highlights of summer was the annual arrival of the funfair – wonderful lights, colours and music. Erected at the Moor end (near church point), "fortunes" (roughly sixpence or so) appeared to be won, lost or spent on the penny arcades and dodgems. Occasionally fights would break out between the local and Byker boys, who would arrive on the Newcastle train and make straight for the fair (or "shows" as we called them). Perhaps "fight" is too strong a description though, because a black eye and torn shirt were about the only major injuries. Fishing at the Needles Eye, well I suppose you could call it fishing with cotton and a bent pin, was great fun – especially catching tiddlers. Eventually we progressed to a hand line of cord with proper hooks and a lead sinker which was swung around until sufficient force was achieved to launch it as far as possible. Barbs on the hooks could create problems for the unwary, and I have memories of my father snipping the eye of a hook off that was embedded in my finger. Some fisherman!

Newbiggin-by-the-Sea beach

Winter brought its own fun, with high seas dashing against the promenade, surf being flung high, wide and handsome. This led to another game for us kids – to watch the timing of the waves and endeavour to race along the promenade between each wave in a vain attempt to stay dry. Explaining to my parents why I looked such a bedraggled mess usually cost me a clip around the ear for telling fibs. Snow brought its own rewards, such as sledging down the pram and disabled pathway, through the railings of the promenade and onto the beach. Once again, though, I found myself in trouble as I arrived home with not only a broken sled but filthy boots. One special Christmas, when I was aged nine, instead of the usual fruit, sweets, and annual, father Christmas had left me a bicycle, black with an eighteen inch frame. Second-hand and small it may have been, but it was mine, all mine! First day out, through the front gate, I ploughed straight into the lamppost that stood not ten yards away. Grounded again, this time with broken spectacles and bloody nose, I at least became familiar with the rudiments of cycle safety.

My bicycle was a regular hell on wheels. At the side of the house was a pathway, or "cut" as we called it, used by pedestrians for a quicker way to the local shops and me on my bike. Only I, trying to mount my bike with a hop, skip and jump would step in some dog muck, curse (you bet I did) at the very unfortunate moment that my mother was collecting coal from the coal house. Another sore behind was shortly to follow. The other abiding memory of the cut was when I was on my way to school one morning hearing my mother shout after me. Turning around, what do I see? My baby sister, clad only in a vest, running after me. What a sight to behold. I must admit I still pull her leg about it even to this day. A lot of the family still lived in North Seaton Colliery at this time and one cousin, Terry (who was of a similar age), and I used to pair up for bicycle rides around the surrounding countryside. Mother used to provide a lunch, usually oxo flavoured crisp sandwiches and a bottle of dilute orange squash. But, say no more. Trouble followed wherever we went. On one occasion flying down a hill called Bothel Bank, with no hands on the handlebars, my front wheel locked into the rear wheel of my cousin's bike and I went straight over the handlebars, earning myself skinned hands, knees, and a sore head.

The years quickly passed with many more ups, downs, scrapes and bruises, followed by sore behinds (especially when I was caught smoking on the beach by one of my brothers who reported the scene to my father). The annoying part, though, was that all my brothers smoked like chimneys anyway; but, there again, they were much older.

∞ ∞ ∞ ∞ ∞

School Days

SCHOOLED THROUGH THE STATE SYSTEM, only later did I realise that this system was solely designed to educate students to the required standard of the job prospects for the areas concerned. The eleven-plus exam, which was supposedly designed to ensure the brightest children has a chance to go to Grammar school, always seemed to favour the mine bosses', doctors' and shop owners' children. Somewhat expectedly, I like many others failed. The Middle school which was situated at the colliery end of Newbiggin was quite some way from home (especially for young short legs), and could be reached either by taking the road or the short cut across the local slag heap (which, of course, was my favourite). Arriving home with filthy shoes and coal dust up to your knees usually meant a clip round the ear from my mother and an early bath.

Household rules didn't change greatly even though we now lived in a posh council house. My younger sister and I were still scrubbed, dressed and ready for bed before Dad arrived home from work. Being quite an ugly duckling, especially with my short trousers, boots, long stockings, spectacles and sleeveless Fair Isle tank-top, I suddenly found myself quite popular (especially with the girls). This I put down to a previously undiscovered talent for writing and directing short plays. When I say "short" I mean the plays were normally written during a play-time and performed over the lunch period in one of the classrooms. I think they were probably more popular because they kept people out of the playground during the normally inclement weather rather than because of my writing ability. Some of the boys, however, didn't take too kindly to my popularity, and being chased home over the slag heaps became somewhat of a regularity.

This period, though, didn't last long, as I was soon old enough to be on my way to the senior school.

The secondary modern school was situated on a bank overlooking Newbiggin bay, and of course the beach was within easy reach. The school itself had no real sports grounds, so pupils were restricted to the gym with the pole vault, high and long jumps taking place in the girls' playground. On sunny days, we also took some of the gym equipment into the girls' playground, where we were allowed to show our physical prowess. Not so Dennis – running and bouncing off the wooden springboard, I completely overshot the high-horse and ended up with coconut mat rash all over the side of my face. On occasion we were taken onto the beach where throwing the cricket ball was the main activity. Apart from the normal Maths, English, Geography, Art, Science and Religious Education lessons, the boys were taught woodwork and the girls cookery (or "domestic science" as it's called these days). I'm afraid my manual skills were not the best, however I found some pride and joy in making a Sea Grass stool that my parents actually bought and used.

Considering my father's prowess in hands-on skills, I can't help but wonder at his disappointment at not having any of his sons being as proficient as he was. Football was played and learnt in the backstreets with the aid of a tennis ball and a gang of raggy bummed urchins chasing after every kick. Scores tended to be in multiples of ten, as were the bruises. It was either football or "British Bulldog," a game that has left me with a scar on my forehead that I still bear today. Schooling, at this time, left us with little choice of job prospects — mine was a choice between the mines or the local coble fishing fleet. However, rebelling against the 'norm' I decided to become a boy soldier (preferably as a bandsman in a Highland Regiment) and found myself at the Newcastle-upon-Tyne recruiting office sitting an entrance exam.

Weeks later I was shocked to find that I had passed the exam whereas the friend I had gone with (who regularly came top in many of the different classes at school) had failed. I still maintain to this day that someone got the papers mixed up! Having arrived at his house full of the joys of spring, I left wondering what I had gotten myself into. I slowly realised that I would have to go on this expedition on my own. Back at the recruiting office I was informed that due to my scores in the exam I should really be going to the Army Apprentice College (then School) at Harrogate, Yorkshire to learn about radio communication. The recruiting Officer painted such a glowing picture that, with my parent's permission, I accepted the Queen's shilling later that same day. Of course, it never entered my head that I would be asking my parents to dig into their hard earned resources to ensure that I arrived at Harrogate in good order with a shilling or two in my pocket. Visions of seeing myself as I had seen two of my brothers, in uniform as they had returned from Korea and Malaya, filled my head. On leaving home with a military second-class, one-way rail warrant and directions to my new school, my great adventure began. Little did I realise that it was the beginning of a career that was to last 25 years. How a life could change in such a short time...

∞ ∞ ∞ ∞ ∞

Army Apprentice School, Harrogate

SO THERE I WAS, one rainy day in April 1960 standing on a platform at Harrogate railway station in my first pair of long trousers a towering 4ft 7 inches tall. With small suitcase in hand, I awaited the call to arms. Ushered not so gently onto a waiting bus full of strangers of roughly the same age, I was full of trepidation at what was to come. An apparent mountain of a man, wearing a battle dress uniform complete with creases as sharp as a razor blade, three brilliant white stripes on each arm, and a red sash across his chest, pointed me onto the bus. His handlebar moustache waxed perfectly into two rapier like points, he waved what looked like a lump of wood around — his regimental pace stick, with which us new recruits would become more acquainted at a later time. On arrival at Uniacke Barracks in Penny Pot Lane (about two miles from Harrogate and completely separated from the main School), we were de-bussed, split into factions, and shown our living quarters. This comprised of a wooden hut (part of a complex we came to know as a spider) with central toilet, and washing and bathing facilities to be shared and cleaned by all. Each barrack room consisted of a separate bunk room used by the room NCO, and around twelve individual bed spaces with a minimal distance between each. Six foot tall metal lockers loomed over iron beds which boasted a criss-crossing metal wire for the bedstead (definitely not bed springs), on top of which sat a thin foam rubber mattress.

Instruction began almost immediately. First: to put and secure the mattress cover (this was there to save the mattress in case of bodily "accidents"); then to make a bed with hospital corners. Pleased with our efforts, the newly-made beds were quickly ripped apart – in order to make the dreaded "bed pack." Sheets and blankets had to be folded to exactly the same length (not too bulky or too thin) while another blanket folded in four (lengthwise) had to encompass the others. This was placed across the bed, and then the first of the folded blankets placed centrally with both folded edges exactly matching. This was followed by the two sheets and the second folded blanket all finally wrapped securely in the long blanket forming an oblong and turned upside down with edges nice and square. This was placed at the top of the mattress with your two pillows (fluffed and with ironed covers) placed neatly on top. The remaining blanket was to cover the mattress (again ensuring hospital corners), any lines having to be centrally aligned. The bed packs became the bane of our lives, mainly because they were never perfect enough for our instructors so they would have to be re-made time and time again. Bed packs every morning ensured that your bed was aired. They had to be re-made prior to the nine o'clock bed check and inspection. Standing to attention in your blue and white striped pyjamas (with draw string), hands, feet, neck and face was inspected for cleanliness before we were allowed to hop into bed for lights out.

Later, on the first day of our arrival, we were formed into some sort of order and shambled off to the gymnasium where we were kitted out with things that were hurriedly stuffed into our kitbags and large packs for carrying back to our billet. Even at 4'7" I was not the smallest boy there by any means, so the conveyance of the kit became something of a comedy. Dumping our kit on our iron bedsteads, we were informed it was time for our first meal. The sight of thirty or forty boys all attempting to swing their right arms in time with their left legs and keep in step with each other must have been a sight to behold, (the left arm was held behind our backs clutching our knife, fork, spoon and one pint – was it china? – mug). How the permanent staff instructors kept straight faces I will never know. On arrival at the cookhouse, we were lined up and given a substantial and nourishing meal (which contained most of the things I'd hated at home!) and told to find a seat. Seating was four to a table (Formica topped with metal chairs) and discussions centred on what type of meat we were eating and who hated what. The greatest problem of course was that none of us boys could understand each other because of the different dialects swimming around the table. My answer to this was to nod and to try and look intelligent. Plum duff and thick custard followed the mains and I don't think I had ever felt so full to the brim as I had that first day. This was so unlike home where my parents had to count every penny to make ends meet for our family of eight. Even so, I was already missing my mother's home baking skills.

After lunch we were informed that we were to be given our first week's pay (ten shillings and sixpence in old money, or fifty-two pence in new!), but first we had to remember our given regimental number. Eight figures to memorise? I was to be known by my last three digits for the rest of my army career (luckily mine was "789"). Pay. Never had I held so much money in my hand, but this was for a regrettably short amount of time since we were once again lined up and marched to the NAAFI (Navy, Army, Air Force Institution) Shop where we were issued with the following: two boot polishing brushes; one blanco brush (a little scrubbing brush); one tin of black boot polish; one tin of green blanco; one tin of white blanco (a compound from the 1880s which was originally for white belts); one tin of brasso; two yellow dusters; a tooth brush; a lock with two keys; and, completing the list, a brass button stick. Total cost? Just over nine shillings. I was left with one and sixpence – or about seven pence today – for the rest of the week. "Ah-ha," I can hear the reader saying, "he's forgotten the toothpaste." Sorry, not so. Away from home we may be, but our mothers still ensured that the basic toilet essentials were incorporated in our bags or suitcases. Why the extra toothbrush, then? It was soon to become an essential part of our cleaning equipment; ideal for getting into awkward corners, such as getting behind brasses on your belt. Instruction and inspection became a daily routine over the next few months – washing, pressing, folding and placing clothes on the correct shelf in your steel locker. Each item folded to the exact same width and placed uniformly one on top of the other. The shelf above your "personal drawer" (where photos of home and other personal items including the odd magazine were kept) was solely for your washing and, yes, shaving kit, which was presented on top of a clean folded towel. Shaving kit? The majority of us barely new even how to hold a razor. However, come evening inspection the odd hair was found and plucked (quite gleefully in some cases) by the inspecting non-commissioned officer.

∞ ∞ ∞ ∞ ∞

Jungle Green Cotton Underpants

ON TOP OF THE STEEL LOCKER was placed your large pack, with small pack above, and a best boot on either side of them. The packs had been scrubbed clean then layered evenly with green blanco and the brass fittings polished to a high shine. Two ammunition pouches, cross belt, bayonet scabbard, web belt and gaiters completed the issue of 58 pattern webbing – and woe be upon you if any of the polish inadvertently hit the blanco (this meant that you would have to scrub that piece of equipment and begin all over again).

The barrack room did not escape from inspection, either. The centre flooring, although wood, had to be polished to a high standard before breakfast at 0700 each morning. This was achieved by firstly dry scrubbing with a special type of brush that had short hard bristles. Usually, one chap helped another by standing on the brush whilst another pulled the brush back and forth. Any dust was quickly swept up, and then liberal amounts of yellow wax type polish (from a rather large can) was placed in irregular lumps over the floor. After this was spread, normally with a rag wrapped around a sweeping brush, the polishing began with an item called a bumper. The bumper consisted of a broom handle with a rather large and heavy weight with a felt type substance attached to its bottom. The manual labour continued – pushing the bumper backwards and forwards over the centre floor until we (perhaps, more precisely, the instructors) were satisfied with the shine.

Our first standard daily military dress was beret, khaki woollen shirt, tie, denim jacket and trousers, gaiters and boots. Of course, one should not forget to add our jungle green cotton underpants to this list, which although quite light did reach down to nearly cover our knees! This was supplemented by a ground sheet which was to be used during inclement weather. The beret: various ways of attempting to shape them were tried, which usually involved transferring them from hot to cold water and then placing them on your head in order to mould them into the required shape. Then, of course, there was the tie – a brown woollen affair that supposedly had to be tied in a Windsor knot. I know the majority of us had never worn a tie before, and some of the attempts, even after instruction, were to say the least, hilarious and woeful. The denim jacket was a wonderful piece of tailoring ingenuity. The buttons were made of a bakelite substance with a small metal loop at the rear. They were pushed through a readymade hole in the jacket and affixed with a small copper ring (similar to a key ring). Who needs fingernails anyway! The jacket tied around the waist and over the top of your trousers using a built in belt system that could be tightened with the use of a crocodile toothed fastener. The denim trousers were an education in themselves. When placing anything in the side pockets care had to be taken since each pocket also allowed easy (and therefore windy) access to the underwear department. Tucked into the tops of your woollen socks and then secured under and over the top of your 58 pattern webbing gaiters, the picture was completed with hob nailed boots. What a sight to behold!

We soon learned about the world of Bull, burning the pimples off your boots (toes and heels of your working boots and all over for your best boots) with the aid of a candle. The trick was to heat the back of the handle of your desert spoon and then quickly apply it with liberal amounts of black polish to the boot in question – but the smell was awful. It was only after you had finally achieved a smooth surface that the hard work began. With one finger tucked into a yellow duster that had first been dipped into water and then a pot of polish (along with large amounts of spittle), one spent hours making small circles on the leather of the boot until a high sheen had been achieved. Here, then, was the origin of the term "spit and polish." Some people achieved the shine quite quickly, while others, like myself, seemed to take an age and was always the subject of some form of criticism. Not everyone could adapt to the tremendous change in lifestyle, and some (although not many) decided enough was enough and asked, and were given, leave to return home.

Our SD or Service Dress uniforms (Circa WWI), which of course were of a khaki serge type material, had jackets with high stiff collars. The two metal clips on the collar which served as fasteners seemed like nothing other than implements of torture. This feeling was enhanced by our shirts, which came with detached collars and studs for fixing front and rear. Of course, no ordinary buttons for us — the use of the button stick soon became apparent. Every button had to be polished with brasso to a very high standard. The stick was to slide under each button to ensure no brasso touched your uniform, creating unsightly black marks.

The weeks passed quickly and the marching, counter-marching, fitness and instruction began to pay dividends. Some of the physical training instructors (PTIs) thought that they were the bee's knees, but looked like nothing more than Dennis the Menace in their red and black striped shirts. Nonetheless, they played their role inspecting each boy in their PT kit of red or white shirt (everyone had to wear the same colour), blue knee length shorts, khaki woollen socks and brown plimsolls. The PTI would also check our necks for any "tidemarks" — the marks of a supposed dirty neck. Those found with such marks were marched straight to the showers to have his neck roughly scrubbed. Some weeks later, no longer looking like the rabble that fell off the bus and shuffled from one place to another, we began to look something like soldiers (some more so than others). It was then that we were introduced to rifle drill.

The rifle drill was taught using the Lee Enfield 303 which weighed around 8lbs and was nearly as big as myself. I soon learned when carrying out the first stages of "sloping arms" not to look down to the right because the front foresight on the rifle had the painful habit of catching you in the corner of your right eye if you weren't careful. About a year later the 303 was replaced with the L1A1 self-loading rifle (SLR), which of course meant a complete change in arms drill. No longer did one pass the rifle across the body from right to left shoulder, or vice versa when the order "slope" or "change arms" was given. Bruised collar bones were a common feature with the 303 but this was replaced by a bruise between the thumb and index finger on the right hand caused again by the foresight when shouldering arms with the SLR.

∞ ∞ ∞ ∞ ∞

'A' Company

TOWARDS THE END OF OUR FIRST TERM an official visit to Hildebrand Barracks was arranged. As the two parts of the school were only half a mile apart, separated by a small woodland and the local YMCA, of course we were marched there. Having been separated into which companies we would be joining, we were first shown our new residences. 'A' company with its yellow shoulder tags for identification was for me and my fellow operators. 'B and D' (red and blue respectively) was for the technicians. 'C' (green) company was for those tradesmen heading for the Royal Engineers. It was a company that was quickly given the unflattering nickname of "Zoo company" by the rest of the school, those who were destined for the Royal Signals.

It was 'B' company who became the envy of the rest of the school because they had the only brick built accommodation. For the rest of us? Yes, you've got it, wooden spiders. Handed over to individual company representatives, we began the royal walkabout. First was the trade training areas, then followed the education centre, gymnasiums, cinema, NAFFI shop and, of course, the central parade ground. The churches we already knew because church parade every Sunday morning was mandatory. Eventually, we all ended up seated in the cinema where we were addressed and welcomed by the camp commandant, who at this time – if memory serves – was Lieutenant Colonel North. He gave us a speech containing the words we were to hear time and again, "You are the future Senior NCOs and Officers of the Army and must conduct yourselves accordingly at all times."

Back at Uniacke Barracks life became full of fevered activity as we prepared for our move to our individual companies. Kit had to be cleaned, folded and packed. And of course, the accommodation had to be left in a pristine condition. The move finally took place a day or so before the summer recess. This, I think, was to ensure we all knew where we had to report and where and with whom we would be bunking. As the day finally arrived it was back onto the green military buses (certainly not built for comfort) to be dropped off at Harrogate train station just before our trains were due. You could tell the new kids on the block by the fact that the majority of us had decided to travel home in our SD uniforms. Given strict instruction from the permanent Staff Instructors not to get involved in any type of gambling with civilians on the way home, we all had various amounts of money that we had saved over the term by the pay staff. Needless to say some of these credits, as they became known, were very helpful to our parents in going some way to pay for board and lodging. In fact, the thing uppermost on every boy's mind (certainly on mine) was to get home, have their mum's cooking and a lovely soft bed to sleep in. It is of such simple things that dreams are made.

∞ ∞ ∞ ∞ ∞

Back at Home

ARRIVING HOME, COMPLETE WITH A MILITARY SUITCASE that seemed to weigh a ton – mainly because it was full of dirty laundry, which my mother seemed to expect and never really commented upon – my initial reaction, after finding out that everyone else was at school or work, was of course to ask what was for tea. Later that day I was the subject of some good-natured ribbing about being a boy soldier, especially from my elder brothers, who took a great delight in comparing my uniform to the one my maternal grandfather had worn in the First World War. However, looking back at photographs of myself in uniform at that time, I now know that irrespective of how proud I felt of myself, I really was a bit of a mess.

The few weeks leave absolutely flew by with me reverting to being the carefree schoolboy of just a few months ago. The only rules and regulations at home, although strictly enforced by my parents, were to be clean, tidy, on time for meals and no late nights for anyone. Dad at this time was still working at North Seaton Colliery and he travelled back and forth at various times of the day (depending on his shift) on his Raleigh bicycle with his shower equipment and mid-shift meal packed in his saddle bag. Thinking back, I find myself amazed at how fit he must have been at that time.

Photographs taken by my Dad in August, 1960
At our home in Newbiggin-by-the-Sea

∽ ∽ ∽ ∽

A Return

WELL, IT WAS BOUND TO HAPPEN. Eventually it was time for me to return to Army life. I suppose most of us recruits must have felt the same way – sorry to leave home with all its comforts, yet excited at facing the unknowns of trade training. In any case, I was once again en route to Harrogate and Hildebrand barracks, this time with my suitcase full of clean and pressed clothes. The smell from the laundry had a dual effect on me. In one way it was a comfort, but in another it was always a reminder of just what I was missing at home. Arriving back in barracks, the normal routine was soon re-established. Beds had to be made and kit folded and put away in our lockers, then, the preparation for our morning 'stables parade' – a hangover from days gone by when horses were the only means of transport. This inspection was again two-fold, firstly to ensure everyone was present and correct, and also that we were all clean and tidy. Imagine my surprise when the Senior NCO taking the inspection was none other than the Sergeant who had first greeted us on our initial arrival, complete with waxed handlebar moustache. Sgt

Lewis, who I believe was in the Prince of Wales's Royal Regiment or 'Tigers' as they were more commonly called, was one of the permanent staff of 'A' Company. Others that come to mind are: Company Sergeant Major Hebden, always remembered for bringing the company to attention with 'Company, company Choo'; Sgt Savage, Royal Artillery, famous for his mistake when checking attendance, shouting 'Redgra, Redgra 13.30,' which was the Hockey pitch and the time we had to be there. Sgt Davis, The Royal Tank Regiment, quiet in his manner. There was also Pipe Major Yule, never to be forgotten. He was a typical, proud kilt-wearing whisky-drinking Scot whose breath, if he got to close, would make your eyes water.

The Pipe Band 1961, Pipey Yule's pride and joy
Notice the wooden and Nissan huts in the background

The funny thing is I can never remember the Officer commanding the company, probably because the only time I saw him was when I was in trouble or ceremonial parades.

∞ ∞ ∞ ∞ ∞

Trade Training: An Education

THE TRADE TRAINING AND EDUCATIONAL instructors were all a mixture of service and civilian people — military personnel always afforded the courtesy of their rank, officers and civilians with the honorific, sir, except when talking to someone else about them, then it was always mister or by their commissioned rank. Two of the first things we were taught were how to type correctly and Morse code. Touch-typing was taught with the aid of a musical metronome, the sound of which still haunts me to this day. A further stage to this was to combine the typing and Morse together under the title of 'Transcription.' Using the old Imperial typewriter, faster Morse speeds could be accomplished even with the heavy clunk when changing from upper to lower case and vice versa. A wide range of radio transmitters and receivers were taught, varying from WWII sets to the Larkspur as they were brought into service. Likewise, the old WB7B post office teleprinter and associated equipment was replaced with the Siemens, which incorporated its own tape relay component. Tape relay – oh yes – learning to read the Murray code: a series of holes punched through a half inch wide white paper tape enabling messages to be sent electronically at a far greater speed than manually.

Unfortunately, not only did we have to learn how to tune and work the radios, we were also taught how they actually worked. First stop, the Electricity and Magnetism (E&M) lessons. What a magic world this was, starting with learning about atoms, protons etc, and delving deep into the mysteries of circuits, valves and things like the resistor colour code. Funnily enough, I can still quote Ohms Law perfectly, even today. Onto Aerials and aerial propagation or Antenna Propagation as it is called today: again, various types of High Frequency (HF) and Very High Frequency (VHF) antennas were taught, along with how to erect them. Lots more theory in the classroom. I never realised how many different ways a radio signal could travel or how the sun could affect communications.

I had thought that school days were to be behind me now that I was in the Army, but no such luck. Education was to be part and parcel of life at Harrogate, and the four main subjects were Maths, English, Current Affairs, and Geography (Science was taken care of through the E&M lessons in trade training). Standards, although not too difficult, were higher than those achieved in civilian Secondary Modern establishments. Examinations were at three standards – the Army Education Certificate (ACE) class three followed by two then onto one. The class one roughly equated to a pass at GCE level. Some of my fellow students were exempt the education classes because they were ex-grammar school, or privately educated, and already held GCE level or above qualifications. Current Affairs became my favourite subject, probably because it was new to me, learning about the various organisations around the world such as the North Atlantic Treaty Organisation

(NATO) and the then South East Asia Treaty Organisation (SEATO). Thinking back, this was probably where my interest in current local and world affairs began, and which could even have birthed my cynical attitude towards politics and politicians!

The instructors/teachers of education were all Senior NCOs or Officers of the Royal Army Education Corps (RAEC) and although coming under the banner of the military, seemed far removed and much more approachable than our normal military instructors.

Physical training was also part of the weekly regime. The Gymnasiums and assault courses all played their part in not only strengthening our bodies but also building our self-confidence and character. Sometimes when training on the assault course a boy would end up hurt and a visit to the MI (Medical Infirmary) room would result. I can't tell a lie, yes, I was once one of them.

Part of the assault course was a water jump where a quick run up was required. I ran, stepped on a loose brick, and found myself half in and half out of the water at the other side clutching my painful private parts. The PTI, being his usual charitable self, pulled me upright and proceeded to bend me over, my head nearly touching my knees and pumped me up and down until I could hardly breathe. On finding out that the pain would not dissipate, I was then ordered to report sick which meant hobbling back to my barrack room, having a shower and packing my small kit (washing kit and pyjamas) then reporting special (out of hours) sick at the company office before making my way to the MI room.

Wednesday afternoon, come rain, hail, or shine, was sports afternoon. Various sports were on offer including the usual: football, rugby, cricket, and hockey. This was very important because inter-company rivalry was prevalent, with points being allocated for practically everything except sleeping. On one occasion cricket was the name of the game, teams were chosen and off we went. During the game, whilst my side were fielding, a ball was struck by an opposing batsman that seemed to go hurtling straight upwards – of course, what goes up must come down. However, this time it came down straight onto the head of a day-dreaming fielder by the name of Dennis (Sarge) Coleman. He sank to his knees and then toppled over. The game was suspended whilst he was checked out (no apparent damage). A sub was brought on and Dennis spent the rest of the game sat on the sidelines chewing a piece of grass.

Indeed, sports were to play a big part not only in the company and school but also inter-school rivalry. I was fortunate in representing my company and school on the odd occasion during my three year apprenticeship: rifle shooting (.22) at AAS Chepstow; boxing at AAS Carlisle; and, gymnastics at home. How I was picked to represent the school boxing team after my performance during the inter-company fights amazes me. I only won my match against a 'D' company boy because of disqualification – he, a senior, fighting me, a junior. Mind you, this glorious victory was only mine after he had first broken my nose with a mighty uppercut. The medic in the MI room caused more pain than the break when he straightened my nose – grabbing it between his fingers and pulling downwards before inserting plugs up each nostril.

∞ ∞ ∞ ∞ ∞

Saturday Afternoons (At the Guardroom)

AFTER EVENING MEAL, time was pretty much our own apart from the usual cleaning of kit and barrack rooms in preparation for the next day. However, that is not to say that there was nothing else to do. Various evening club activities were available, which of course we were invited to take part in. The activities ranged from the rifle range to music under the instruction of Pipey Yule. Of course, I shouldn't forget the evening study classes, here. These usually appeared if you were a little behind in some of the theory or homework. Sometimes, if we could afford it, a trip to the garrison cinema was in order, which just left enough time to get back – showered and ready for bed before lights out at ten thirty. As a junior you were allowed down town (Harrogate) on a Saturday and Sunday afternoon but only wearing the School's dark blue blazer, complete with the apprentice school badge on the left breast pocket, and grey flannels. Of course, the majority of us had no such clothing. However, this was not a problem as the school had an arrangement with a local store whose representative would turn up at the YMCA to take all the necessary measurements and arrange the paperwork so that a certain amount could be deducted from your weekly wages to pay for the purchase. Hire purchase by arrangement – that shop must have loved each new intake.

So, there you were, suitably booted and spurred ready for Saturday afternoon downtown. First stop, though, was the guardroom in order to book out, but that was not before you'd been inspected and given the rules of expected behaviour etcetera. This included the time of the last bus to get you back before the nine o'clock deadline. Too young to partake of alcohol, which you wouldn't have been served anyway in blazer and flannels, meant you spent the majority of time walking 'round and visiting the odd café and, of course, the wonderful Women's Royal Voluntary Service (WRVS) canteen and rest room where beans on toast and a comfy armchair were more than welcome. The WRVS ladies, God bless them, mothered us and listened to all our little moans and groans about life in the Army. The WRVS house, on a side street in Harrogate, was a refuge from all our aches and pains. Needless to say the sight of apprentices in blazers and flannels wandering around their town meant a certain amount of abuse was forthcoming from some of the town's youth which rarely amounted to anything more than a bit of name calling.

If you stayed behind in the barracks during the weekend (usually due to lack of funds) – or on a normal evening – you were allowed to wear civilian clothes. These usually comprised of a pair of jeans and some form of sweatshirt; anything for comfort really.

Dialects became less of a problem the longer we were together, and a sort of cosmopolitan language began to evolve – a complex mixture of north, south, east and west which I found carried on throughout my military career (as did the comradeship which the British forces always seemed to have in spades).

Discipline, as you might imagine within a military environment, was quite strict and the favourite punishment handed out to those who were termed defaulters (I must admit yours truly had his fair share) was restriction of privileges. Invariably this meant not only being confined to barracks but reporting to the guardroom at various times to ensure your attendance. Reporting only took place in the evenings during the week as trade training time was sacrosanct, but on the weekends you had to report throughout the day and evening. Never a dull moment allowed, you reported first in your best kit to be inspected and then, if any work needed to be carried out, you were given a short period of time to get back to your barracks, change into denim overalls, and report back again. The work details could vary from cleaning offices or the guardroom to painting kerbstones in an alternate black and white pattern. However, with no work detailed, one of the favourite pastimes of the guardroom staff was the mannequin parades. This involved the defaulters racing backwards and forwards to their barracks to change into various items of clothing which were then inspected. Each time something was found to be amiss, and so you had to race back to barracks, correct the fault, and race back to the guardroom only to be told, "Okay. Now change into ..." And the cycle would begin all over again. Standing on the guardroom veranda in your PT kit in the middle of winter was no fun because you knew, looking at the snow, ice and slush, that the likelihood was that you were going to be using a shovel and brush within the near future. The only good thing about it was that the army blue PT shorts were so long that they covered the knee.

∞ ∞ ∞ ∞ ∞

The Move to Chellaston

TOWARDS THE LATTER END OF MY SECOND TERM I received a letter from my parents informing me that, with the aid of a council house exchange procedure, they were moving to a village just outside of Derby called Chellaston. Once again I found myself in the company office, this time not in trouble, but to change my next of kin details. This had to be done so that when my leave pass was approved my rail ticket would be to Derby station and not Newcastle. My eldest brother, Raymond, had moved to Derby with his wife Audrey some time before, and of course this led to the remainder of the family calling him mummy's favourite.

End of term finally arrived and of we went on our various home journeys, this time in civilian clothes and me with directions on how to get from Derby to Chellaston. Was I in for a surprise, on arrival in Chellaston? I was greeted by the thickest, dankest pea-souper of a fog that really meant you could not see the end of your nose clearly. Eventually, I found myself in the correct street, Peters Road, but could not make out any house numbers so it was a case of knocking on a stranger's front door and asking directions to my parent's house which was directly opposite. Oh, how strange fate is, little did I realise that a girl living in the house I had knocked at was not only to become my girlfriend Patricia but also my wife, who I married in 1965 and still puts up with me to this day.

Patricia on our wedding day
Outside St Peters Church, Chellaston

Chellaston, what a complete contrast to North Seaton and Newbiggin! It was surrounded by fields, people farming and working on the land instead of mining. One of Chellaston's claims to fame is the story that Robin Hood was born in a manor house in the village, although mentioned a lot in and around the 1800s no positive proof of this has ever emerged. One thing that has been proven, however, is that a local sheriff at the time of Hood was known to have some affiliation with the area.

The village itself was a complex mix of private, council, and farm housing. The private housing was mainly situated along the main road through the village and up some side streets. These were the large posh homes, and many of them of course were complete with drives. The farm and council properties, although completely different in style, often sat side by side because of the farms close proximity. Three public houses, two butchers, a co-op, post office, petrol station/garage, and a couple of other small privately owned shops and newsagents completed the picture. That said, I must not forget St Peters Church (C of E) where my wife was taught bell ringing and where we eventually married. This was one of four different places of worship in the village. Catholic, Methodist and Baptist religions were all catered for, but time has seen the Baptist Church close through lack of membership.

*The exterior of St Peters Church
where my wife and I married in 1965*

There were other means of employment within easy reach in Derby. The three main ones were Rolls Royce, Qualcast, and British Rail. My father, much to my surprise, had gained employment as an overhead crane driver at the Carriage and Wagon works at British Rail; my mother, as ever, had found herself a job in one of the local public houses (the Corner Pin) serving behind the bar.

For my parents, this sojourn in Chellaston only lasted two years as my father missed the North east and longed to go back home. Yet, for me, I was split between my new girlfriend and knowing that if I didn't return with my parents to Newbiggin it would upset them greatly. I can only say the return journey to the North East was not a tremendously happy event for me.

At this time my wife-to-be had left Derby Art College and gained employment as a seamstress with Sketchley and Co. a dry cleaning and garment repair emporium in Derby city. On my next leave, my Dad, realising just how much I missed my girl, arranged for me to travel to Derby to pick up some nonexistent equipment he had mistakenly forgotten at our old house in Chellaston. How well he knew me! On arrival in Derby the first thing I did was go to Sketchley to see Patricia (or 'Fred' as she became known later in life) only to be greeted with the words 'Oh, it's you. You're like a bad penny, always turning up.' I actually ended up staying with my future parent's in law for a couple of nights – mending bridges and ensuring the courtship was back on track. I returned home a very happy person indeed.

The Corner Pin public house

∞ ∞ ∞ ∞ ∞

Back to Work

AS TIME PASSED and we slowly became more proficient in our trades and military ethos, our experiences were gradually widened. Map reading and use of the compass became quite a necessity especially when trogging across the Yorkshire Moors (irrespective of weather conditions). Moors? Some of the hills there seemed to climb forever. Usually split into groups of three or four, and given map referenced staging points (RVs), we would carry our food, clothing, water and sleeping equipment in our backpacks. Of course the route and compass bearing was usually confirmed by the whole squad and differences resolved before we moved off. Memories of sleeping in a two-man bivvy (small tent) in our green slugs (military sleeping bags) still haunt me today. Careless pitching of your bivvy could, and did, result on occasion in you waking with a rather damp and wet feeling. The sleeping bags, although quite warm and comfortable, were only waterproofed on the bottom and anyone will tell you when it rains in Yorkshire it really rains (from the heavens!).

Woken at first light by cows mooing right next to your head is not conducive to a good temper. However, this usually abated soon after a hot brew and breakfast. I must admit that some of the local farmers and their wives did take pity on the wet and bedraggled messes that used to cross their land – and not only did they offer us the use of their barns but sometimes even a hot meal. A debt of thanks is owed by myself and many other apprentices to those wonderful Yorkshire people.

∞ ∞ ∞ ∞ ∞

Training Complete

1963 ARRIVED AND WITH IT MY LAST TERM AT AAS HARROGATE. What a term this was to be, preparing us for the big wide world. Trade training complete, apart from a few final exams, we would soon be classified as A3 Telegraph Operators (a trade name that was to change a few times during my career). Then the day arrived when we were to be issued with our very own Battle Dress (BD), which, as we had learned, meant much ironing and pressing of new creases. For some reason we were handed over to Company Sergeant Major (CSM) Maguire, an Irish Guardsman (whose wife worked in the NAAFI shop and was also the subject of much adoration by the apprentices). His role was to ensure that our drill for our pass-off parade was beyond reproach. Mornings, afternoons and evenings, drill and inspections followed drill and inspections until finally the day arrived that the whole school stood on parade as a showcase for our parents and families. Smart as a carrot with my new posting in my pocket and a tear in my eye, we marched off, no longer a boy soldier but a Signalman of the Royal Corps of Signals. Life was about to change with a vengeance once again for me. But that, as they say, is another story...